Create and Share | Thinking Digitally

Unboxing and Reviewing Online

By Adrienne Matteson

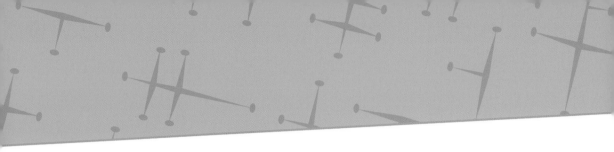

Published in the United States of America by Cherry Lake Publishing Group
Ann Arbor, Michigan
www.cherrylakepublishing.com

Series Adviser: Kristin Fontichiaro
Reading Adviser: Marla Conn, MS, Ed., Literacy specialist, Read-Ability, Inc.
Book Designer: Felicia Macheske
Character Illustrator: Rachael McLean

Photo Credits: © AVAVA/Shutterstock.com, 5; © Rawpixel.com/Shutterstock.com, 7; © maxim ibragimov/Shutterstock.com, 9; © Pair Srinrat/Shutterstock.com, 13; © Africa Studio/Shutterstock.com, 21

Graphics Credits Throughout: © the simple surface/Shutterstock.com; © Diana Rich/Shutterstock.com; © lemony/Shutterstock.com; © CojoMoxon/Shutterstock.com; © IreneArt/Shutterstock.com; © Artefficient/Shutterstock.com; © Marie Nimrichterova/Shutterstock.com; © Svetolk/Shutterstock.com; © EV-DA/Shutterstock.com; © briddy/Shutterstock.com; © Mix3r/Shutterstock.com

Library of Congress Cataloging-in-Publication Data has been filed and is available at catalog.loc.gov

Cherry Lake Publishing Group would like to acknowledge the work of the Partnership for 21st Century Learning, a Network of Battelle for Kids. Please visit *http://www.battelleforkids.org/networks/p21* for more information.

Printed in the United States of America
Corporate Graphics

Table of
CONTENTS

CHAPTER ONE
Thinking Outside the Box 4

CHAPTER TWO
Begin with the Box 8

CHAPTER THREE
Getting the Word Out 14

CHAPTER FOUR
Branding: Taking Your Channel to the Next Level 18

GLOSSARY 22
FOR MORE INFORMATION 23
INDEX 24
ABOUT THE AUTHOR 24

Thinking Outside the Box

Imagine you just got a new toy that you are very excited about. Right now, it is trapped inside a box. But soon, it will be in your hands! Taking something new out of its box and seeing it for the first time is called unboxing.

People create videos of unboxing products. These videos become product **reviews**. People try out the product and give their opinion about it. A good unboxing video is both entertaining and helpful. It gives kids a chance to see what new toys and games look like in and out of the box. And it helps parents decide what to buy.

Some unboxing videos have over a million views!

There are thousands of YouTube channels for unboxing videos. Some of the most popular videos are done by kids. Unboxing videos can be easy to make but hard to make stand out. In this book, you will learn what makes a good unboxing video and how to give helpful reviews. You will also get tips for making your videos and channel stand out. It's time to think outside the box!

Read Reviews

Reviews are helpful. Sometimes we read reviews to make decisions. We go on Yelp to decide where to eat. We go on Goodreads to decide whether or not to read a certain book. We check Amazon reviews before purchasing something. With a trusted adult's permission, read reviews on different sites. What makes a review good? What makes it bad?

What is your favorite thing to unbox?

CHAPTER TWO

Begin with the Box

First impressions matter. Companies put a lot of time and care into how their products are **packaged**. A good unboxing video begins with the box itself.

Set up your camera in a spot where you can easily film all sides of the box. You will want a **tripod** or another hands-free way to keep the camera steady. If you are filming with a smartphone or tablet camera, you might also want a microphone so your video has better sound. Make sure you have enough light. Your **audience** will want to see the box and what's inside clearly.

Try to use natural light and make sure fans and
other things that make small noises are turned off.

Now it's time to film. Hit the record button and start the unboxing by telling your audience what you hope or expect the item inside the box will do. Next, carefully open the box and begin to take out what's inside. Talk about each thing that you pull out. After you have everything out of the box, try it out. If it needs to be built, put it together. If it needs to be plugged in, plug it in.

Once you have it ready to go, it's time to review. Your review should describe the product and include what you think about it. As you try out the product, talk about what you like and don't like. Decide if the product does what it is supposed to do. Be honest and respectful, and let your personality shine!

Don't forget to edit your video! You can do this using various apps on your phone or computer. Perhaps you want to speed up the unboxing or the building of the product. You can use a time-lapse app. Or maybe you want to add background music. There are plenty of apps you can use, including Animotica, FilmoraGo, and iMovie.

If your video is fun to make, it will be fun to watch.

Research

To become good at something, sometimes you need to do a little research. This might mean studying the successes and failures of others in order to learn from them. With permission, watch a handful of unboxing videos. Try to find at least one unboxing video with more than 1 million views and one with less than 1,000 views.

Use this list while watching the videos. Then, make a plan for how you will make your own video.

- What are things you like and dislike?
- What are the differences between the videos with more views and fewer views?
- Are the videos loud enough? Are they too loud?
- Look at the lighting. Can you see everything clearly?
- Are there places where they speed up the video or cut to a later time?
- Were the reviews clear? Did the reviewers make you want to purchase the item? Why or why not?

It's okay if you don't like the product.
Be honest but respectful in your review.

CHAPTER THREE

Getting the Word Out

You've made your unboxing video. Now it's time to share it with the world! The most common place to put your videos is on YouTube. But there are other choices. Many people put unboxing videos on Instagram, Vimeo, and TikTok. Remember that you must be 13 years old to be on social media **platforms** by yourself. So you will need an adult you trust to help you create an account and post your videos.

To get started, decide which video platform you'd like to use. Then, create an account. Next, pick a name for your channel. The name should reflect what kind of videos you make. It should not include your full name. The next step is to **upload** your video. Sometimes it can take a very long time for a video to upload. So it might be a good idea to do this right before bedtime. After that, there are some things you need to do to help your video reach its audience.

YouTube is part of Google. If you or one of your parents, already have a Google account, you don't need to create a new one. But, if your Google account is for school, you should make a new one. You don't want your unboxing videos to be on a school account.

- Give your video a title that clearly describes what it is. Use words that people would search. For example, "Unboxing New Nintendo Switch!" uses words that explain what the video is about.

- Write a short description of the product. Include information your viewers will need if they decide to buy it. This might include the price and a website that sells it.

- There will be a place for you to mark if your video is for kids or not. If you check "yes" here, more kids will be able to see your video.

- Use **hashtags** with keywords like "unboxing" and "review." Also use the names of the product and the company that made it. So your hashtags might look like #unboxingreview #unboxingnintendoswitch #reviewingnintendoswitch.

- Your safety is important. Always ask an adult to help you post videos and check that all of your information is safe. Remember, don't include personal information like your full name or where you live.

Creating Great Descriptions

Practice writing video descriptions for your video. The descriptions do not need to be long. They should have no spelling errors and include all of the important details. Think about what you would want to know if you watched this video on another channel. Write two to three video descriptions and show them to a friend or family member. Ask them to proofread and help you choose the best description.

CHAPTER FOUR

Branding: Taking Your Channel to the Next Level

You did it! You created an unboxing video and uploaded it to your channel. Now everyone can see it. But how do you get more people to see it? There are a lot of ways to create your own **brand**, or a way for people to recognize and know you online.

A good place to start is with the way your channel looks. Platforms like YouTube allow you to add artwork to your channel to personalize it. You can also add custom pictures, or thumbnails, to appear in your videos. Branding this way with thumbnails will make your videos easier to spot and remember!

My GREAT Reviews

Unboxing videos can be expensive because you have to buy a product before you can unbox it! So at first, make unboxing videos with gifts you receive and are very happy about. Let's say your family gets something exciting like a new video game console. Ask if you can make a video while the whole family unboxes it.

Some popular reviewers receive free products to review. If a company does send you a product to review, be sure to thank them. In your review video, you should say that the company sent the product to you for review. And be sure to send the company a link to your review, especially if you loved the product. Your review should still be your honest opinion, even if you got the product for free.

If your videos get a lot of views (10,000 or more), you might be able to get some products to review for free. Ask an adult to help you reach out to a company that has products you would like to review. Tell the company who you are and share a link to your videos. Explain to them which product of theirs you would like to review and why. Many companies set aside products to send to reviewers. You might get to be one of them!

Reviewing new products is a lot of fun. It's especially fun if they are free!

Creating Art

Coming up with artwork for your channel can be tricky. Think about colors you love and what your channel is all about. Draw a few pictures that might look good. Go back to the unboxing videos you looked at in chapter 2. Look more closely at the pictures they used to make their channels stand out. Do they give you some good ideas? Which one is your favorite?

GLOSSARY

apps (APS) computer programs that perform a special function

audience (AW-dee-uhns) the group of people you hope will watch your videos

brand (BRAND) the fonts, designs, and styles you use that make your videos sound like you

first impressions (FURST im-PRESH-uhnz) the feelings or opinions you have the first time you see something or someone

hashtags (HASH-tagz) words or phrases that start with the symbol # that help with online searching

packaged (PAK-ijd) how a product is placed or packed inside a box

platforms (PLAT-formz) social media websites and apps, like Instagram, TikTok, and Facebook

reviews (rih-VYOOZ) opinions written or given to help others make a decision about a product

time-lapse (TIME-laps) when a slow action is sped up in a video

tripod (TRYE-pahd) a camera stand with three legs

upload (UHP-lohd) to send information to another computer over a network

BOOKS

Lovett, Amber. *Creating Digital Videos*. Ann Arbor, MI: Cherry Lake Publishing, 2020.

Minden, Cecilia. *Writing a Review*. Ann Arbor, MI: Cherry Lake Publishing, 2020.

WEBSITES

YouTube—Kids' Toys
https://www.youtube.com/user/TheEducVideos
Discover new toys alongside two YouTube stars.

YouTube—TheToyReviewer
https://www.youtube.com/user/TheToyReviewerVideos
Unbox toys with Brittany.

INDEX

artwork, 21
audience, 8, 10

boxes, opening, 8–10
branding, 18–21

channel, 15, 18–21

descriptions, 16, 17

editing, 11

Google, 15

hashtags, 16
honesty, 13, 19

Instagram, 14

keywords, 16

music, 11

packaging, 8
platforms, video, 14–15
product reviews, 4, 7, 10
    honesty in, 13, 19

research, 12

safety, 16
social media, 14

thumbnails, 18
TikTok, 14
time-lapse app, 11
titles, 16

unboxing videos
    branding, 18–21
    first impressions, 8–13
    reviews, 20
    sharing, 14–17
    uploading, 15
    what they are, 4–7

videos, unboxing. *See*
    unboxing videos
Vimeo, 14

YouTube, 6, 14, 15, 18

About the AUTHOR

Adrienne Matteson is a middle school librarian in Atlanta, Georgia. When she is not teaching her students to be good digital citizens, she is knitting, singing, and serving the community.